"The secret of change is to focus all of your energy not on fighting the old, but on building the new."

– Socrates

Made in the USA
Columbia, SC
05 July 2024

38128315R00057